DAYS THAT SHOOK THE WORLD

THE **FALL** OF THE **BERLIN WALL**

9 NOVEMBER 1989

Pat Levy

HODDER
Wayland

an imprint of Hodder Children's Books

DAYS THAT SHOOK THE WORLD

Produced by Monkey Puzzle Media Ltd
Gissing's Farm, Fressingfield
Suffolk IP21 5SH

First published in 2002 by Hodder Wayland
An imprint of Hodder Children's Books
Text copyright © 2002 Hodder Wayland
Volume copyright © 2002 Hodder Wayland

Series Concept: Liz Gogerly
Commissioning Editor: Alex Woolf
Editor: Jason Hook
Design: Jane Hawkins
Picture Researcher: Lynda Lines
Consultant: Michael Rawcliffe

Cover picture: Celebrations on the Berlin Wall on
9 November 1989 (Camera Press/ERMA).
Title page picture: East German guards prepare to defend the Brandenburg Gate as
celebrating West Germans gather on 10 November 1989 (AKG London/F Gaul).

We are grateful to the following for permission to reproduce photographs:
AKG London 9, 10, 11 bottom, 15 (East German Press), 19 bottom, 21, 23 top, 26,
27 (F Gaul), 36 (Dieter E Hoppe), 37 bottom (Dieter E Hoppe), 46; Associated Press
16 left (Kreusch), 20, 43 top (Jan Bauer), 43 bottom (Thomas Kienzle); Camera Press 14,
18, 23 bottom (ERMA), 24 (ERMA), 29 top (ERMA), 30 (ERMA), 40 (Sven Simon);
Corbis 32 (Robert Maass), 37 top (Gregor Schmid), 38 (Robert Maass); Corbis/Bettmann
Archive 8, 11 top, 12, 13, 19 top; Popperfoto/Reuters 22, 25 right, 29 bottom, 34,
35 top, 42; Topham Picturepoint 6, 7, 16 right, 17, 25 (AP), 28 (AP), 31 (AP), 33 (AP),
35 bottom (AP), 41; UNHCR 39 (LeMoyne). Artwork by Michael Posen.

Printed and bound in Italy by G. Canale & C.Sp.A, Turin

British Library Cataloguing in Publication Data
The fall of the Berlin Wall. - (Days that shook the world)
1. Berlin Wall, Berlin, Germany, 1961-1989 - Juvenile literature
I.Title
943.1'55'0879

ISBN 07502 3563 2

Hodder Children's Books
a division of Hodder Headline Limited
338 Euston Road, London NW1 3BH

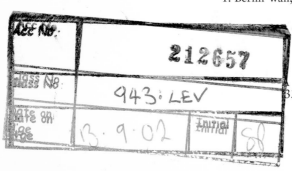

CONTENTS

East German soldiers stand guard on top of the Berlin Wall, built to prevent East Berliners escaping to West Berlin.

O N THE AFTERNOON OF 9 November 1989, a meeting of the East German government was taking place in East Berlin. No one present realized that this meeting would have extraordinary consequences. It would, in fact, lead to a moment that changed world history – the fall of the Berlin Wall.

By 1989, Germany had been a divided country for over forty years. West Germany and East Germany were two separate countries, each with its own government and its own capital city. The borders between the two countries were closed. Berlin, deep inside East Germany, was also a divided city. A concrete barrier, the Berlin Wall, ran through it. Those living on the eastern side of the wall were citizens of East Germany. Those living on the other side of the wall were citizens of West Germany, even though their city lay within East Germany. The wall had been built to prevent East Germans crossing from East to West Berlin.

Now East Germany was facing a crisis. Its government, like most of those in Eastern Europe, had been under the control of the communist Soviet Union for decades. But the Soviet Union was going through a period of reform under its leader Mikhail Gorbachev. In the past few years, Gorbachev had been relaxing the strict laws by which communist governments ruled. East European countries had begun to make similar reforms. One of them, Hungary, now had a more liberal government – which had decided to open its borders to the West. For the first time in many years, people were being allowed to leave Hungary and travel into Western Europe. East Germans had begun leaving their country in large numbers – pouring through Czechoslovakia into Hungary, and then crossing the border into Austria.

At the meeting on 9 November the leader of the East German government, Egon Krenz, tried to deal with the crisis. He announced that a new law would allow citizens to travel or emigrate to the West, but only after they had applied for a passport and a visa. It was thought that forcing people to make this application would slow down the rate at which they were leaving.

Gunter Schabowski, a high-ranking politician, turned up late for the meeting. His copy of the new law was pushed over the table to him and he was told to make it public. That evening, Schabowski met journalists in East Berlin for a press conference. He was to outline recent changes in the work of the government. Schabowski pulled out his last piece of paper, scanned its contents for the first time and read it aloud. Without realizing it, he made an announcement that prepared the way for the fall of the Berlin Wall – and for the reunification of Germany.

A Moment in Time

At 6 pm on 9 November 1989, in a stuffy East Berlin hall, a press conference is taking place. Gunter Schabowski, the government spokesman, makes a closing statement: 'Today, the decision was taken to make it possible for all citizens to leave the country through the official border crossing-points. All citizens can now be issued with visas for the purpose of travel or visiting relatives in the West. The order is to take effect at once...' Journalists shout: 'When? How soon?' Schabowski scans his note, then replies: 'It just means straight away.' The room empties.

An East German celebrates on 11 September 1989, as he crosses the Hungarian border into Austria and the freedom of the West.

Soldiers from the Soviet Union hoist their country's flag over the Brandenburg Gate in Berlin, to celebrate victory over Germany in the Second World War.

A Divided Family

" The main house was in the Soviet zone while some of the fields were in the British zone. The border literally divided the property. Aged seventeen, my father hid a suitcase on a horse-drawn cart and drove west across the border on family property, leaving his parents behind. In the following forty years he was allowed to return only twice – for a maximum of three hours each time – for their funerals. "

Author Oliver August, in Along the Wall and Watchtowers, *remembers how the partition of Germany divided the farmland where his father was growing up.*

THE SECOND WORLD WAR came to an end in Europe in May 1945, with victory for the Allies – led by the USA, the Soviet Union and Britain – over Nazi Germany. Long before this, the Allies had considered the problem of what to do with a defeated Germany. At first, as a way of making sure that Germany could never again become too powerful, they had proposed breaking up the country into a number of smaller states, each with its own government. But this idea had been replaced by a plan to partition, or divide, Germany between the USA, the Soviet Union, Britain and France. This was to be a temporary partition, with each of the Allies in military control of its own zone, until a new and trusted administration could once again govern a united Germany. At a conference in London in 1944, the borders of these zones had been agreed upon.

It was logical for the Soviet Union to be given control of the eastern part of Germany. The Soviet army had advanced from the east, pushing back the German army which had invaded and tried to conquer the

EUROPE IN 1945
Km 0 300 600
Miles 0 200 400
Moscow
BRITAIN
NETHERLANDS
London
Amsterdam
BRITISH ZONE
Air corridors
Berlin
POLAND
GERMANY
Brussels
Bonn
SOVIET ZONE
Warsaw
SOVIET UNION
BELGIUM
Paris
FRENCH ZONE
US ZONE
Prague
CZECHOSLOVAKIA
LUXEMBOURG
Vienna
FRANCE
Bern
SWITZERLAND
AUSTRIA
Budapest
HUNGARY
ROMANIA
BLACK SEA
Bucharest
Belgrade
MEDITERRANEAN SEA
ITALY
YUGOSLAVIA
BULGARIA
Sofia
Rome
ALBANIA
Tirana
GREECE
TURKEY
Athens

Germany and Berlin were both partitioned between France, Britain, the USA and the Soviet Union.

BERLIN DIVIDED
Km 0 5 10 15
Miles 0 5 10
FRENCH SECTOR
Fegel
SOVIET SECTOR
BRITISH SECTOR
Gatow
Tempelhof
US SECTOR

Soviet Union. In two world wars, the Soviets had seen their country invaded from the west. Now they wanted to ensure their future security by making countries such as Poland and Czechoslovakia (today divided into the Czech Republic and Slovakia) into 'buffer states' on their western border.

The American, British and French zones would be situated in the western half of Germany. A decision had also been made in London in 1944 about Berlin, the German capital, which was located in what would become the Soviet zone. It had been agreed that the city should also be divided into four sectors, with each of the Allies controlling a sector with its military force.

Berlin, like most German cities, was in ruins by the end of the Second World War. Its people were starving. As the summer of 1945 turned into winter, and the Allied forces settled into their sectors of occupation, arguments developed over how supplies should be moved around the city. More importantly, a political struggle between the Soviet Union and the USA began, as each tried to gain influence over the divided and shattered country of Germany. This struggle would turn into what became known as the Cold War.

As the USA and the Soviet Union developed into the two great superpowers of the world, the city of Berlin would become a world stage for the conflict between them.

In the summer of 1945, Berlin's starving citizens receive potatoes from the occupying forces.

THE PARTITION OF GERMANY would last for over forty years, largely because of the development of the Cold War. This conflict set the powers of the West – led by the USA, Britain and France – in opposition to the Eastern Bloc – the Soviet Union and the other communist countries of Eastern Europe. Each side had opposing views about how their countries' economic and social systems should be organized. The Cold War never developed into open and armed war between the two superpowers, but it sometimes came very close to doing so.

Each side in the Cold War wanted to ensure that the part of Germany it controlled would develop in the way that it wished. For the Soviet Union this meant communism, which required authoritarian rule and an economic system controlled by central government. For the USA it meant democracy and capitalism, an economic system based upon competition for profit between private companies.

In 1948, a new currency called the Deutschmark was introduced into the American, British and French zones of Germany, but not the Soviet zone. This made it clear that the two sides would not agree on an economic system common to all of Germany. When the new currency was extended to the western half of Berlin, the Soviet leaders responded angrily by blockading that half of the city. Over two million people in the west of Berlin relied on 12,000 tonnes of supplies brought in daily along the one road and one rail route that the Soviet Union allowed through its zone of Germany. In June 1948, the Soviet Union closed these routes and cut off the electricity supply. In a month, the people in the west of Berlin would begin to starve.

A West Berlin policeman checks cars leaving East Berlin in February 1949. The division of the city into two halves had already begun.

An American plane flies into West Berlin in May 1949, carrying much-needed supplies.

A little girl in West Berlin in June 1949, celebrating the arrival of fresh milk after the lifting of the blockade.

Germany, with Bonn as its capital. Five months later, the eastern part of Germany and the eastern part of Berlin became the German Democratic Republic. This was known as East Germany, and the eastern part of Berlin became its capital. The country of Germany was now divided into two separate states, and divided Berlin had two names: West Berlin and East Berlin. The beginnings of the Cold War had redrawn the map of central Europe.

The leaders of the western powers came to the city's rescue by mounting a massive airlift. Many different aircraft, including ramshackle old bombers, carried supplies into the city. By the spring of 1949, 8,000 tonnes of food and other supplies were being airlifted into Berlin every day. In May, the Soviet Union accepted defeat and lifted the blockade.

Also in May, the western part of Germany and the western part of Berlin were named the Federal Republic of Germany. This became known as West

An Iron Curtain

Winston Churchill, Britain's prime minister during the Second World War, made a speech in 1946 at Fulton, Missouri, USA. He drew attention to the way post-war Europe was dividing into two opposing groups of countries, and said: 'From Stettin in the Baltic to Trieste on the Adriatic an iron curtain has descended over the continent.' By the end of the Berlin blockade, this was indeed seen to be the case. In time, this iron curtain would take on a very physical form in the shape of the Berlin Wall.

On 16 October 1961, an American soldier faces an East German officer across the white line that divided Berlin.

A White Line

Between 1949 and 1961, Berlin was a divided city but there was no wall separating its two halves. Indeed, in some places in 1949 there was only a white line painted on the road to show where the border was. Buses and trains ran freely across the whole city and so did telephone lines. Depending on which side of the city citizens lived, they were required to pay for train tickets and settle such things as telephone bills in either East German or *West German* currency.

EVEN AFTER EAST GERMANY and West Germany closed their border in 1952, people could move freely across the whole of Berlin. But the political divisions of the Cold War were already clear in the city. Each side of Berlin had its own police force. Each side also had its own army. The people of West Berlin lived in a city surrounded by the East German state, and to reach West Germany they had to travel 190 kilometres by one of three ways: air, train or road. There was only one railway line and one road, with no garages or rest facilities between West Berlin and the West German border. Commercial flights into West Berlin could only be provided by American, British and French airlines. These airlines could only fly through East Germany along three air routes or 'corridors'. These corridors had been agreed between the four wartime allies in 1946, and had been used to airlift supplies during the Berlin blockade.

Although West Berlin was physically isolated inside East Germany, West Berliners did not live the kind of restricted life that many people imagined. In fact, the effect of the Cold War resulted in some advantages for West Berliners. Western powers wanted to make their part of Berlin a showcase for capitalism and democracy. American money was used to help rebuild West Berlin, and West German companies were encouraged to set up their factories there.

East Berlin developed in a different way. Under the communist system of East Germany, East Berlin provided its citizens with guaranteed employment, low rents and free medical care. But there were also disadvantages. There was not the same level of wealth. The economy was not supported as generously as in West Berlin, and the city began to fall into disrepair. In June 1953, the poor conditions in East Berlin led to an

uprising when thousands of workers went on strike in protest at their working conditions. The strikes ended only after troops from the Soviet Union were sent in to restore order.

Berlin remained at the centre of the continuing Cold War. Politicians from both sides talked about reuniting Germany. But Berlin not only remained divided, it became a symbol of the differences between the two superpowers. In 1958, Nikita Khrushchev, the Soviet leader, criticized the USA for placing nuclear weapons in West Germany. He also called for the whole of Berlin to become the capital of East Germany. In contrast, the American president John F Kennedy spoke in July 1961 of West Berlin as 'the great testing place of Western courage and will'.

West Berlin police take an East Berlin citizen into protective custody after he crossed the border during the riots of 1953.

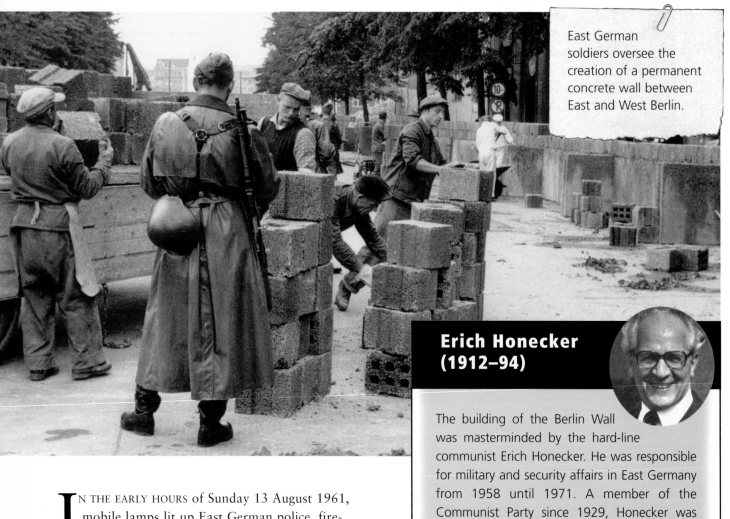

East German soldiers oversee the creation of a permanent concrete wall between East and West Berlin.

Erich Honecker (1912–94)

The building of the Berlin Wall was masterminded by the hard-line communist Erich Honecker. He was responsible for military and security affairs in East Germany from 1958 until 1971. A member of the Communist Party since 1929, Honecker was elected to the politburo in 1958. He became leader of East Germany in 1971, and ruled the country until 1989, when he was forced to resign. In 1992, he was tried for manslaughter for ordering guards to shoot people trying to escape over the Berlin Wall. His ill-health prevented the trial's completion, and Honecker was instead exiled to Chile.

I N THE EARLY HOURS of Sunday 13 August 1961, mobile lamps lit up East German police, fire-fighters and customs officials as they unfurled huge rolls of barbed wire in the streets of Berlin. Armed soldiers formed a line along the border, standing with their backs to West Berlin. Civilians watched, amazed, as armed vehicles, trucks and heavy machinery drew up. The East Germans now began building what would become known as the Berlin Wall. This barrier would eventually surround the whole of West Berlin.

The government's motive for building the Berlin Wall was an urgent need to stop large numbers of East Germans leaving their country. The border between East and West Germany had been closed since 1952, but there was nothing to prevent East Germans travelling to East Berlin and crossing over freely to West Berlin. They could then choose either to live there or be flown out to West Germany. Between 1949 and 1961, around 15 per cent of East Germany's population of 17 million people had made their way to West Germany.

During the first half of 1961, the number of East Germans leaving through Berlin had reached alarming proportions. Nearly 20,000 had left in March alone. Many of these were skilled workers and professionals, and as a result the East German economy was in serious danger of collapse. The higher standard of living in West Germany was an attraction for many East Germans. They were also worried by the build-up of American and Soviet troops in the two halves of Germany. The Cold War was heating up, and people feared that the borders might soon be closed.

Berliners awoke on 12 August 1961 to the dramatic news. On the radio and across telephone lines, word spread that the barrier being built through the city was no temporary measure. The entire 43-kilometre boundary between East and West Berlin was being closed, permanently. At 6 pm, West Berliners gathered on their side of the Brandenburg Gate, a famous landmark just inside East Berlin. They carried placards saying: 'There is only one Germany.' With growing anger, the crowd surged forward, chanting and hurling stones across the wire. East German soldiers armed with machine guns confronted the protesters. Some soldiers, realizing how close their colleagues were to opening fire, yelled across to West German police to hold back the crowds. The East German soldiers then used water-cannon to disperse the protesters. They defused a situation that could easily have become a blood-bath.

In the coming weeks, the barbed wire barrier across Berlin would be developed into a concrete wall. It would be twenty-eight years before this wall was removed.

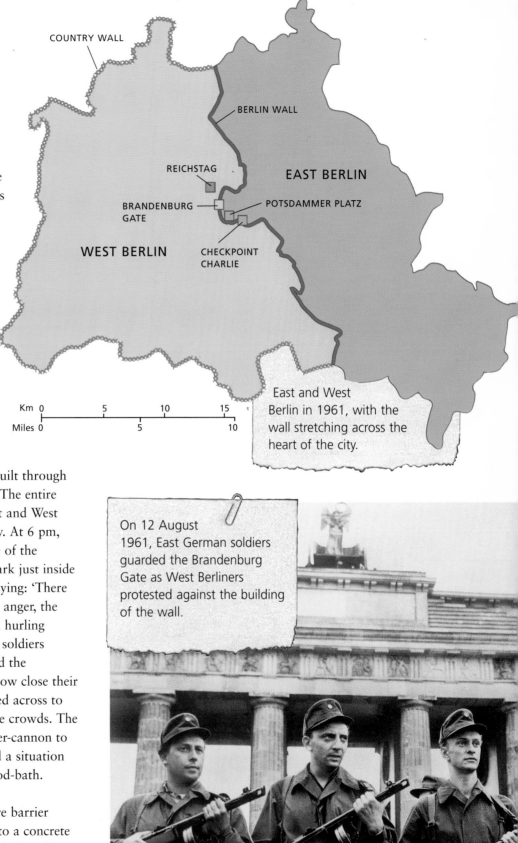

COUNTRY WALL

BERLIN WALL

REICHSTAG

EAST BERLIN

BRANDENBURG GATE

POTSDAMMER PLATZ

WEST BERLIN

CHECKPOINT CHARLIE

Km 0   5   10   15

Miles 0   5   10

East and West Berlin in 1961, with the wall stretching across the heart of the city.

On 12 August 1961, East German soldiers guarded the Brandenburg Gate as West Berliners protested against the building of the wall.

On 28 October 1961, American tanks (foreground) and Soviet tanks confront each other at Checkpoint Charlie. The crisis came about after American diplomats were denied access to East Berlin.

IN THE DAYS FOLLOWING 13 August 1961, as the barbed wire began to be replaced by blocks of concrete, it became clear that the USA and its western allies would not confront the Soviet Union over the building of the Berlin Wall. Demonstrators on the western side of the wall marched with placards that read: 'Betrayed by the West'. But the USA's President Kennedy was forced to accept the situation because, as he wrote, 'only war could reverse it'.

In October 1961, it seemed that war might come. East German guards denied some American diplomats access to East Berlin. The small disagreement grew out of control, to the point where Soviet and American tanks were facing each other at a crossing-point known as Checkpoint Charlie. It was one of the most perilous moments in the Cold War. But Kennedy and Khrushchev, the leaders of the two superpowers, pulled back from armed confrontation.

An elderly woman prepares to jump to the freedom of the West from her fourth-floor apartment.

At first, some East Berliners found ways to cross the divided city. The border splitting the city followed traditional divisions between the old districts of Berlin, and the wall was formed in places by the walls of houses. Some people's homes stood in East Berlin, while their front doors opened into West Berlin. East German guards boarded up these doors, only for whole families to escape through windows using ropes of knotted bed-sheets.

Between 1961 and 1989, about 5,000 people escaped from East to West Berlin. Balloons and pedal-power aeroplanes were used more than once; tunnels were dug and people were smuggled across the border inside industrial machinery. One of the more amazing escapes was arranged by a circus manager. He managed to smuggle acrobats across the border one by one in a trunk. Another extraordinary escape involved a man whose wife had not been allowed to join him in West Berlin. He made a day trip to East Berlin with a woman who resembled his wife, stole her identity papers and used then them to return with his real wife. The unfortunate other woman spent two years in jail in East Berlin, and the man was sentenced to seven months imprisonment by a West German courtroom.

Many people lost their lives in their attempts to cross the Berlin Wall. In June 1962, an East German border guard was shot and killed by a man escaping. Two months later, a young man named Peter Fechter was shot by East German guards while attempting to escape, and was left to bleed to death in sight of American troops. He was the first of 192 people who would die trying to escape across the Berlin Wall. Their deaths were regular reminders of the grim reality of the wall, and the deadly nature of the Cold War.

The Wall 1961–89

Total border length surrounding West Berlin	155 km
Border between East and West Berlin	43 km
Concrete wall	3.6 m high, 106 km long
Wire-mesh fencing	66 km
Anti-vehicle trenches	105 km
Number of watch towers	302
Number of bunkers	20
Persons succeeded in crossing the wall	c. 5,000
Persons arrested in the border area	c. 3,200
Persons killed on the wall	192
Persons injured by shooting	c. 200

The body of Peter Fechter, the first person to be killed attempting to cross the wall, is recovered by East German guards.

With the wall dividing families, people stood on ladders to wave to their relatives across the barrier.

IN THE YEARS FOLLOWING the building of the wall, Berliners got on with the task of living under its shadow. The West German government encouraged its citizens to live in West Berlin by lowering rates of income tax compared to the rest of the country. Housing was also subsidized in West Berlin, and young people living there were not required to do military service – which was compulsory in the rest of West Germany. The government pumped money into West Berlin, and subsidized hotel rates were used to encourage people to visit the city. As tourists flocked into West Berlin, the Berlin Wall found itself in a new role – as a tourist attraction.

For East Berliners, life also began to improve. They enjoyed excellent healthcare, crêche facilities, virtually free public transport, full employment and subsidized food and rents. With skilled workers no longer deserting to the West, output from factories rose dramatically in the 1960s. Many East Germans genuinely believed that their communist system was fairer than the capitalism of West Berlin, and they grew proud of their achievements.

But East Berliners lacked some of the key freedoms enjoyed by West Berliners: freedom of speech, free elections and the right to leave their country and travel freely to the West.

While Berliners were settling into life with the wall, Soviet attitudes towards the rest of Eastern Europe were hardening. The building of the wall was not the only sign that force was necessary to impose the Soviet system of government. In 1956, 3,000 people had been killed when Soviet troops were sent to put down a revolt against the communist regime in Hungary. In 1968, reforms took place in Czechoslovakia, in what became known as the Prague Spring. The leader of the government, Alexander Dubçek, tried to introduce what he called 'communism with a human face'. But his moves towards democracy were ended abruptly in August 1968, when Soviet tanks rumbled into Prague.

In Prague, in August 1968, crowds surround the Soviet troops brought in to suppress the reforms known as the Prague Spring.

In the 1970s, it was the turn of the people of Poland to campaign for more freedoms. Their calls for reform were led by the trade union movement known as Solidarity. But this movement was also put down with force, this time by Poland's own troops. It was clear that the Soviet Union and the communist governments of the Eastern Bloc were not yet ready to tear down walls of any kind.

A Moment in Time

On 26 June 1963, President John F Kennedy, during a visit to express American support for West Berlin, stands on the balcony of the city's town hall. He looks out over a quarter of a million West Berliners, and beyond them to the wall. It has become a symbol of the divisions of the Cold War. To cheers from the crowd, Kennedy makes a famous speech that ends: 'All free men, wherever they may live, are citizens of Berlin, and therefore, as a free man, I take pride in the words *Ich bin ein Berliner* (I am a Berliner).'

President John F Kennedy delivers his famous speech at the Berlin Wall on 26 June 1963.

Some 120,000 demonstrators march through the East German city of Leipzig on 17 October 1989, demanding greater freedom.

THE POLITICAL CONDITIONS THAT would eventually bring down the Berlin Wall began to develop in 1985, when Mikhail Gorbachev became leader of the Soviet Union. He wanted to introduce reform to the Soviet Union, but for it to remain a communist state. Gorbachev introduced two striking new ideas: *glasnost* – freedom of information, free speech and free elections – and *perestroika* – economic reform within communism. Significantly, he also began to withdraw Soviet control from the political systems of other Eastern Bloc countries. Gorbachev felt that they should experience reform without Soviet interference.

In June 1989, Gorbachev made his first visit to West Germany and was greeted by crowds of supporters. What newspapers across Europe were calling 'Gorbymania' was an expression of hope that the Cold War might be coming to an end. When asked about

the Berlin Wall, Gorbachev said: 'The wall could disappear once the conditions that created the need for it disappeared.' He was saying that the fall of the wall was dependent on the end of the Cold War.

Also in June, Poland elected a non-communist government. Nothing like this had happened before in an Eastern Bloc country under Soviet influence. Even more dramatic was Hungary's decision on 10 September 1989 to allow East German refugees to cross the Hungarian border into Austria. Many East Germans had travelled to Hungary during the summer and waited at the border in the hope that this would happen. Now they drove across Austria and into West Germany. The Iron Curtain was going up.

The East German government was facing a crisis. Protesters gathered in the city of Leipzig calling for an end to laws which prevented them from travelling freely into the West. In the East German city of Dresden, young people took over the railway station in an attempt to ride out of the country on a train.

In October 1989, Gorbachev visited East Berlin to help celebrate the fortieth anniversary of the founding of East Germany. Also present was Erich Honecker, the hard-line communist leader of East Germany. Honecker was strongly opposed to Gorbachev's reforms. At a torchlight parade intended to celebrate East German power, marchers chanted 'Gorby, Gorby, save us!'

Honecker had lost control of the situation. Having also lost the support of Gorbachev, he was forced by the politburo to resign. They replaced him with Egon Krenz, another hard-line communist who was, however, prepared to make limited changes. By November, a million people were marching in the streets of East Berlin, demanding that the borders were opened. It was time for the wall to come down.

Mikhail Gorbachev (1931–)

Mikhail Gorbachev joined the Communist Party in 1952, and became local party leader in Stavropol in 1970. He was appointed Agricultural Secretary in 1978, and became a full member of the politburo two years later. In 1985, he became leader of the Soviet Union. Gorbachev hoped to revive the failing Soviet economy by changing some aspects of communism while maintaining its basic beliefs. He also abandoned the Soviet policy of intervening in any communist state which needed help to maintain communism. This was an essential step in the eventual fall of the Berlin Wall.

The parade to celebrate the fortieth anniversary of East Germany on 7 October 1989, which was watched by Gorbachev and Honecker.

40 JAHRE DDR

East Berliners climb up onto the Berlin Wall on the night of 9–10 November 1989.

O N THURSDAY 9 NOVEMBER 1989, the press conference described at the beginning of this book took place. The government's vital detail that travellers would need to obtain visas was lost in the excitement of the main news – East Germans were to be allowed to cross the border. Journalists ran from the room, most to the nearest telephone. Within the hour, East German television was broadcasting the news that the barriers along the Berlin Wall were opening. The switchboards were jammed by East Berliners unable to believe what they were hearing. When West German television also started to broadcast the news, people stepped out into the frosty Berlin night to see if it was true. At the wall itself, no one had given the East German guards new orders. They stayed at their posts as the crowds gathered at the wall's crossing-points.

9.00 pm A few people approached the guards at the crossing-point on Invaliden Strasse. The guards told them they would need to obtain passports and visas before they could cross.

9.30 pm A middle-aged husband and wife went to the Bornholmer Strasse crossing and asked to be allowed through. The guard there had heard the news on his radio. He let them through but made them promise to come back to East Berlin later on! The crowd of East Berliners that had gathered behind them recovered from their amazement and approached the guard. He waved them all through.

10.30 pm Programmes on West German television were interrupted as news crews arrived at the crossing-points. Word spread that

East Germans in Trabant cars queue to cross the Glienicker Bridge into West Berlin.

people were going through at Bornholmer Strasse. The guards at the other official crossing-points, confused and without proper orders, heaved up the barriers – some of them rusted into place from disuse – and allowed the crowds through. On the other side of the wall they met West Berliners who had come to greet them carrying whatever they could pick up as gifts: hot drinks, flowers and champagne.

11.59 pm By midnight, the border guards had received official orders to open the gates. There were queues of East German Trabant cars at each crossing-point, filled with East Berliners. Some were still wearing their pyjamas. A street party broke out in West Berlin. Just after midnight, a young man climbed up on his friend's shoulders and clambered onto the wall. Only hours before he might have been shot. Now the top of the wall became a sea of dancing figures, spraying champagne over the crowds below. Someone brought out some fireworks, and gaudy rockets began soaring over the celebrations.

A narrow escape

" We didn't get any instructions from our superiors, none. Only, 'observe the situation'. We tried many times to speak to our superiors, but nobody got back to us. You have to bear in mind that our soldiers were fully armed on this day as always. And they had one order [shoot anyone who tries to cross]. "

Lothar Stein, a guard on duty that night, recalls how the celebrations might have turned to tragedy. Quoted in the CNN television documentary The Wall Comes Down.

On the night of 9 November 1989, a celebration began on top of the Berlin Wall.

THE PARTY LASTED ALL through the early hours of Friday 10 November, with about 40,000 East Berliners crossing to the West. Shops had stayed open all night, and many East Berliners went window-shopping. When they were tired they simply went home or slept in the parks. The wall, three metres wide in some places, was crowded with dancers. All along it, there was the sound of hammers and crowbars chipping away at the stone. The noise expressed years of anger that the wall should ever have existed.

3.30 am The East Berlin newspaper *Berliner Zeitung* was handed round on the streets bearing the headline: 'The wall is gone. Berlin is Berlin again!'

9.00 am At Eberswalder Platz, East Berlin, bulldozers demolished a section of the wall to make a new crossing. People decorated the gap with flowers, and West Berliners flocked to it to welcome the 'Ossis', as they called the East Berliners. At one crossing-point, British soldiers in charge of the barrier erected trestle-tables on which they put tea-urns and plates of biscuits. In West Berlin, children were given the day off school.

Since 1 September 1987, the West German government had been offering visitors from East Germany a 'welcome to the West' gift of 100 Deutschmarks. In 1989, this was worth about $55 or £35. It was enough to buy a few luxuries: fruit, sweets or some perfume. Long lines of East Berliners now formed at banks and money-changers in West Berlin to collect their money.

In the evening, East and West German border guards worked together to hold back the crowds so that no one was injured in the crush. Some of the guards swapped hats. As they carried small children to safety,

West Berliners begin to tear down the wall that had divided their city.

The Century's Business

" We walked everywhere, watching whole slabs of the wall crash down, seeing flurries of celebration, awkward reunions, people falling silent. Then dawn came up. We breakfasted groggily on brandy, coffee and pastries outside a cafe, under a crystal blue sky… it soon became clear that a lot of the century's business, and a dreadful period in Germany's history, was being concluded. "

Henry Porter, an English student at the time, remembers the night of 10 November 1989. Quoted in the Guardian, 2 November 1999.

they complained to their former enemies about the foolish behaviour of the crowds. News had travelled across the world and people from all over Europe had joined the throngs at the wall, cheering every East German Trabant as it sputtered across the border.

In the first twenty-four hours after the border was opened, only about 1,200 'Ossis' registered for permanent residence in West Berlin. For most people the opening of the wall was a symbol of change in their own country, not a chance to escape from it. One woman recalled her experience of a few hours in the West: 'Going to West Berlin was as good as going to Australia for me. It was just as far away. But now I've been there and back while my children were home in bed.'

A West Berlin policeman (left) offers a helping hand as his former enemy, an East Berlin guard, steps through a break in the wall.

An East German guard reaches up to hand a flower to West Berliners sitting on top of the wall.

East German vehicles with water-cannon protect the Brandenburg Gate as the wall is constructed in 1961.

Achtung!
Sie verlassen jetzt
West-Berlin

The Brandenburg Gate

The Brandenburg Gate was built in 1788–91, as a symbol of peace, after Prussia – a German state – had intervened in the Netherlands to prevent a revolutionary uprising. But from such beginnings, it became a symbol of German nationalism and military power. It was at the Brandenburg Gate that Adolf Hitler staged many of the Nazis' political rallies. The great arch, with its statue of a chariot drawn by four horses, was destroyed in the Second World War. It was rebuilt in 1958, and in 1989 was at the heart of the German demonstrations supporting reunification. Sadly, ten years later it became a meeting point for neo-Nazi demonstrations.

IN THE DAYS SURROUNDING the momentous opening of the Berlin Wall, one particular place attracted the attention of protesters. Demonstrators calling for the reunification of Germany gathered at the famous arched gateway called the Brandenburg Gate. Until the Berlin Wall was built, the gate had been part of a main road in Berlin and traffic passed through it every day. Then, in 1961, the wall was built in front of it, leaving it in East Berlin, and the gate was closed to both East and West Berliners.

On the night of Friday 10 November 1989, West German protesters climbed up onto the top of the Berlin Wall opposite the Brandenburg Gate. There was a 'no-man's land' on the eastern side of the wall, which had been created to make it impossible for escapees to even reach the wall without being shot. Now, East Germans crossed this no-man's land and were pulled up onto the wall by the West German protesters.

The East German border guards had the strange experience during the day of stopping people getting into East Berlin rather than out of it. As the crowds built up around the Brandenburg Gate, more troops were sent in to keep demonstrators in order. Some 300 armed East German troops formed a barrier in front of the gate while lorry-loads of reinforcements waited behind it.

From time to time, East German troops fired water-cannon at people dancing on the wall. Some West Berliners climbed over the wall and dropped down into the no-man's land in front of the Brandenburg Gate. Every so often the guards drove them away. At 3 am, protesters broke off

a piece of the wall in front of the gate, and both West and East German troops hurried in to clear the area.

For weeks after the Berlin Wall opened, crowds gathered around the gate, with car headlights lighting it from both sides. They called for its opening, until finally it was announced that the gate would be officially reopened on 22 December 1989. The news was met with mixed feelings by Germany's neighbours. Both Britain and France saw the event as part of a resurgence of the kind of nationalism which had led to the rise of the Nazis in the 1930s. President François Mitterrand of France – a country invaded and conquered by Nazi Germany – refused to attend the ceremony.

East German guards once again defend the Brandenburg Gate. This time they stand on top of the Berlin Wall, on 10 November 1989, as West Germans gather to celebrate its fall.

On Saturday 11 November, a crane lifts out an entire section of the wall to make a new crossing-point.

ON THE AFTERNOON OF Saturday 11 November 1989, the West Berlin football team Hertha Berlin was playing. East Berliners, who for twenty-eight years had only been able to watch their team play on television, were offered free tickets. As the crowds flooded into West Berlin, more breaches were made in the wall to accommodate them. At one place in the wall the crowd knocked over an entire three-metre-high section of concrete and physically carried it away.

Overnight, maps of the city had been printed to help the Ossis find their way around. The Kurfurstendamm,

West Berlin's main shopping area, was closed to traffic. Soup kitchens had been set up, and shops, bars and restaurants handed out gifts to the visitors. Banks ran out of cash for the 'welcome to the West' handouts, shops ran out of fresh fruit and the price of bananas rose by 10 per cent. One chain of supermarkets had lorries driven up to the crossing-points to give out bags of sugar.

In the evening, the Berlin Philharmonic Orchestra performed a free concert in West Berlin, playing the music of the great German composer Ludwig van Beethoven. Outside of the city the borders between

East German soldiers with pieces of the Berlin Wall, which were packaged up and sold to tourists.

Over the following months the wall was completely demolished by Prem and other contractors, and the pieces carted away for road-building projects. In the twenty-first century, only one tiny section of the wall has been preserved as a reminder of its history.

East and West Germany had opened in places, and queues of cars waiting to cross stretched for 60 kilometres. All over Germany, beyond the joyful and exuberant partying at the wall, families met relatives they had not seen for twenty-eight years. Many had not expected to see each other ever again. By midnight, 2 million people had crossed into West Berlin. Most of them simply returned home to their families and jobs the next morning.

On Sunday 12 November, the West German government got over its own shock at what had happened and began making plans. It announced that East Germans could travel free on public transport and could gain free entry to all public entertainment.

In the following week, bits of the wall were being hawked as souvenirs, and builders made a profitable trade out of demolishing further sections to allow more freedom of access. One West German demolition contractor, named Winifried Prem, said he had always dreamt of 'how my crushing machine could crumple and pulverise the wall'. Now he realized his dream.

A Moment in Time

Potsdammer Platz – once a bustling square at the centre of Berlin – has stood silent and empty for twenty-eight years, lit only by the beams of searchlights. At 8.30 am, 12 November 1989, an entire section of the wall here is lifted out by crane. On either side of the gap stands a man. Walter Momper, the mayor of West Berlin, and Erhart Krack, the mayor of East Berlin, are waiting to formally greet each other. As the area is cleared, the two men step forward and meet in the square. They shake hands. Walter Momper announces that Potsdammer Platz will regain its former identity as a square at the heart of the reunified city. A roar goes up from the crowds.

Mayors Walter Momper and Erhart Krack shake hands in Potsdammer Platz, on 12 November.

29

West German chancellor Helmut Kohl lends his support to the East German elections in March 1990.

Free Elections

In March 1990, free elections were held in East Germany for the first time, to elect a national assembly and government. The party that won was supported by Chancellor Kohl's party in West Germany. An East German expressed his voting intention: 'Kohl's is the party of money, so I'm voting for it.'

THE BERLIN WALL HAD symbolized the divisions of the Cold War, which had seen the German people split into two separate nations and kept apart by force. The tearing down of the wall represented the end of this Cold War conflict, but it also raised a vital question. What would happen now to the two Germanys?

Even before the end of November 1989, the chancellor of West Germany, Helmut Kohl, announced his government's wish to reunite the two Germanys. New elections were due in West Germany in December 1990, and Kohl wanted to win these elections by leading the way in the reunification of Germany. The USA supported the idea, with the condition that a united Germany must become part of the Western system of democracy.

The possibility that the two parts of Germany would once again form a united country alarmed some people. For many East Germans who had taken part in the demonstrations in Leipzig and East Berlin before the wall fell, reunification was an unexpected result. Like Gorbachev, many of the demonstrators were committed communists. They just saw no reason why communists should not have free elections and freedom of speech, as well as the things they were used to having, such as subsidized housing, free healthcare and full employment. On their visits to the West, East Berliners saw fresh fruit, electronic goods, designer labels and perfumed soap. But they also saw things that were not so attractive, such as the enormous gap between the wealthy and the poor.

West Germans, especially West Berliners, also saw problems ahead. Their streets were filled with noisy, polluting East German Trabants or 'Trabbie' cars.

Their shops were crowded. Levels of petty crime had soared, and there was a shortage of housing and food. East Germany had a number of serious economic and environmental problems. Its industries were so old-fashioned that some machinery was bought up immediately by museums. Industry had also not had the same laws for waste disposal. Any West German business which chose to form links with an East German company faced huge expense in cleaning up the environmental pollution.

Kohl foresaw many of these problems. Very quickly after the wall fell, he also proposed a common currency, assuring the people of both halves of Germany that there would be no loss to either side. A special rate would be set between the two currencies so that East Germans, whose currency was so much weaker, would not have their savings wiped out by a poor exchange rate.

East Berliners protest against reunification.

In July 1990,
Mikhail Gorbachev and Helmut Kohl signed agreements allowing the united Germany to become a free and independent state.

BY THE TIME OF East Germany's free elections in March 1990, it had become generally accepted that Germany would be reunified. It had also become obvious that West Germany, with its economic power, would be in charge of events. East Germany would be a willing but less powerful participant.

The meetings that led to the reunification of Germany took place between May and September 1990. The two Germanys negotiated their future with the four powers who had agreed to the partition of Germany and Berlin after the Second World War: the USA, the Soviet Union, Britain and France. According to treaties signed after the war, these four powers still had certain rights over Germany. From the negotiations emerged the 'Two-Plus-Four' Treaty. The West German foreign minister Hans Dietrich Genscher, who came up with the term, explained: 'We had to avoid giving the impression that the Four were negotiating about

Germany. This is how the word order in the title of the conference came about: Two plus Four, not Four plus Two.'

The Soviet Union played a crucial role in deciding the nature of a new, united Germany. In July 1990, at the same time as the German currency union was taking place, Gorbachev and Kohl held talks. As a result, Gorbachev agreed that a united Germany should be a free and independent state. This meant the country would have the right to join NATO (North Atlantic Treaty Organization) – the military alliance, led by the USA, that had opposed the Soviet Union during the Cold War.

Kohl announced, at a press conference on 16 July 1990, that a reunified Germany would be part of NATO. This caused almost as much astonishment as the press statement made seven months earlier, when

Schabowski had announced that East Berliners could cross the Berlin Wall. Not only was the Cold War over, but it felt to some as if the USA had won. On 3 October 1990, a new Germany came into existence, in which East and West Germany, and East and West Berlin, were combined.

Not everyone welcomed the prospect of a unified Germany. France's President François Mitterrand and the British prime minister Margaret Thatcher had opposed the idea. They shared a fear among Germany's wartime enemies that a powerful German state might once again dominate Europe.

For Germans themselves, there were immediate problems. Those from the east had no experience of competing for work. They also had none of the technical skills needed to compete for jobs.

Immigrants from all over Eastern Europe were also seeking a better life in Germany. This led to the growth of pro-Nazi groups, who wished to keep their new country for themselves.

A Changing Berlin

" For me and other members of my generation it was comfortable not to have… Germany any more. So I could say I had nothing to do with the Germany of the concentration camps and the Holocaust. The Federal Republic I grew up in was not Germany, only West Germany… over all those years I had built up an… anti-German identity. And then these refugees arrived calling out 'Deutschland' from the train windows. "

Sociologist Wolf Wagner on how reunification forced the post-war generation to face up to their country's past. Quoted in Unchained Eagle: Germany After the Wall *by Tom Henegan (Reuters, 2000).*

Another moment of history at the Brandenburg Gate: a firework display to celebrate German reunification on 3 October 1990.

Stasi secret police struggle with a demonstrator protesting at the celebrations of East Germany's fortieth anniversary on 7 October 1989.

IN THE MONTHS FOLLOWING the fall of the wall, there were many revelations about how East Germany had been run. Evidence emerged of corruption among the politicians who had once controlled the state, and of the brutal behaviour of East Germany's secret police, the Stasi.

In former East Berlin, people attacked the Stasi offices, and took away any secret files that had not been hidden or destroyed. These files revealed that there had been 85,000 full-time employees of the Stasi, and over half a million paid informants. These informants had spied on their neighbours and workmates, and reported any suspicious behaviour to the Stasi. The Stasi had kept files on the activities of a third of all East German citizens.

All Germans were now permitted to see their own files. Some had the unpleasant shock of finding out that close family members had been spying on them. Where it was possible, Stasi informants and employees were now sacked from their jobs. But informing had been carried out on such a huge scale that most informants escaped punishment. Ex-members of the Stasi also found it easy to accuse their enemies of having once worked for them. Justice was hard to achieve, and a great deal of bitterness was aroused.

Other revelations showed up the double standards of the former East German leaders. Although they claimed to despise Western luxuries, many had enjoyed goods unavailable to the public. Erich Honecker, East Germany's leader from 1973 to 1989,

An employee at Stasi headquarters in Berlin looks through the files that have become open to public inspection.

Learning the Truth

" I was brought up and educated by that regime. I never knew anything else. I truly believed it was right. I trusted my party and my government and I genuinely thought the Stasi were doing a good job to protect society – until two or three years ago when the stories of their brutalities began to leak out, but at first I just didn't believe them... Now I feel bereft. But I still believe in the socialist ideal. "

An East German journalist describes how the revelations affected him. Quoted in Germany and the Germans *by John Ardagh.*

had owned a hunting lodge with a staff of twenty-two people, as well as an island retreat in the Baltic Sea. He and his wife had even made secret trips to Paris to go shopping. Such luxuries were normal for political leaders in the West, but Honecker was a communist leader who claimed to believe in equality. Senior politicians in Honecker's government were also accused of selling arms to foreign countries in order to fund their private bank accounts.

Officials had been responsible for ordering the killing of people who tried to escape across the Berlin Wall. But they could not easily be prosecuted, as they had acted under East German law. As the 1990s progressed, some former ministers and members of the Stasi were brought to trial, but little was proved. Honecker, now an elderly man, was arrested in Moscow and sent back to Germany. He was charged with corruption and manslaughter, but was allowed to leave Germany when he became ill. He went first to Russia, and then to Chile where he died in 1994.

Erich Honecker is extradited from Moscow to Germany to stand trial for his part in the deaths at the Berlin Wall.

IN THE FIRST YEARS after the wall fell, there were many problems in Germany. Berlin in particular needed massive redevelopment. Large areas of housing in East Berlin were in poor condition. The old centre of the city, where the wall had been, had become a no-man's land. The city's leaders also had a unique problem: they had to co-ordinate two healthcare systems, two education systems, two public transport systems and so on.

In 1961 East Berlin's underground railway, known as the U-bahn, had been cut off from the West for fear that East Berliners might escape through the tunnels. In 1989, fifteen stations were reopened, along with roads and bridges. But telephone lines were very limited and those in East Berlin were outdated. In the months following reunification, little could be done to modernize them.

In the arts there were more than two of everything. The governments of East and West Berlin had poured money into the arts to show off their city. There were three opera houses, ten orchestras, twenty-seven theatres and three world-class museum complexes. These had to be sorted out, into what was and was not essential. This generally meant that jobs had to be cut in the overstaffed theatres of East Berlin.

Wildlife along the Wall

For twenty-eight years, a strip of land 90 metres wide and 43 kilometres long had been left undisturbed in the heart of Berlin – where the wall had stood. Much of this land ran along railway lines and through parks. When the land-mines, barbed wire and the wall itself had been cleared away, biologists discovered that the area contained unexpected flora and fauna. There were 1,432 species of plants and animals along the strip, five times more than the average for other cities. Kingfishers were well established there, as were plants that usually grow in warmer climates. It is thought that seeds and insects were accidentally brought in along the railway lines and grew in the undisturbed environment. Sadly most of this environment has now disappeared in the huge rebuilding schemes of the city centre.

Inside the Theater Unter den Linden, one of East Berlin's many theatres.

This new dome was built on top of the Reichstag in 1996, after it became Germany's new parliament building,

The main debate to concern the German government was whether Berlin should now become the country's capital again. The city still had the grand old buildings of pre-war Germany. These included the Reichstag, or parliament building; St Nicholas Church, built in 1200; many beautiful museum buildings; and the Brandenburg Gate. Berlin also had a huge area of free land where the wall had stood, which would make a perfect site for grand new public buildings. However, Berlin also brought with it memories of the Nazi era, and of the kind of nationalism that had once threatened to destroy the whole of Europe.

The other option was the city of Bonn. It had been the capital of West Germany, and Germany's allies in NATO were familiar with the city as a place where they discussed trade, European integration and other peacetime events. However, Bonn was located in the west of the unified country. It would make East Germans feel even more unimportant.

In 1991 it was finally decided to make Berlin the capital. The decision was made even though it meant moving all the government offices and the parliament building from one side of the country to the other.

Past and present in Berlin: a replica of the world's first traffic signals of 1924, outside the Red Box where plans for the city's future are put on display for the public.

Mikhail Gorbachev was declared *Time* magazine's 'Man of the Decade' for the 1980s.

WHILE GERMAN REUNIFICATION gathered pace, the rest of the world watched open-mouthed as changes it had never thought possible took place in Europe. The fall of the Berlin Wall had signalled the end of the Cold War, and the consequences of this momentous event reached far beyond the borders of Germany.

In Eastern Europe, communist governments quickly gave way to democracies. Czechoslovakia, Poland and Hungary made the transition to democratic government with little violence. But in Romania it was a very different story. The communist leaders of Romania refused to give up their power without a struggle. There was a coup, and the communist dictator Nicolae Ceasescu and his wife were executed by firing squad.

The peaceful end of the Cold War was Mikhail Gorbachev's greatest achievement, but he and his country were to pay a very high price for this extraordinary event. The most unexpected consequence was the collapse of the Soviet Union itself. Non-Russian states within the Soviet Union, such as Lithuania and Latvia, began calling for their independence. A Russian leader, Boris Yeltsin, supported them and challenged Gorbachev's position as leader of the Soviet Union. On Christmas Day 1991, Gorbachev accepted that the Soviet Union had come to an end, and resigned as its leader. Yeltsin then became head of the new state of Russia.

Events such as the fall of the Berlin Wall seemed to many to represent not just the end of the Cold War but the victory of the USA in that conflict. Some

Russians, without wishing to resurrect the Cold War, felt a sense of humiliation and defeat at the loss of their country's superpower status. Others, like Boris Yeltsin, wanted Russia to embrace capitalism in ways that Gorbachev had never intended. As the new millennium began, Russia was striving to cope with the frantic pace of its economic reforms, and to find a new role for itself in the world.

Many people believed that the end of the Cold War would create a period of peace in Europe. This did not happen. The former Yugoslavia, in particular, has suffered many crises. Yugoslavia had been created as a country at the end of the First World War, and it held together states including Bosnia, Croatia and Serbia. In 1991, as the Soviet Union broke up, these states began to demand their own independence. Within months, a war had broken out between different ethnic groups, marked by terrible atrocities.

Celebrate or Forget?

The Germany that emerged after the fall of the Berlin Wall faced new problems and challenges. So too did the new independent states that emerged after the end of the Cold War. This German joke, from 1999, reflects the mixed emotions felt in Germany and Europe:
Customer: 'Waiter, what wine do you recommend for the tenth anniversary of German unity?'
Waiter: 'That depends...'
Customer: 'On what?'
Waiter: 'Well, do you want to celebrate or forget?'

Quoted in Along the Wall and Watchtowers *by Oliver August.*

Refugees in 1999 flee from fighting in Serbia, in the former Yugoslavia. The end of the Soviet Union brought war and misery to the region.

Soviet tanks end the Prague Spring of 1968. If the Berlin Wall had not fallen, would tanks have crushed the protests in East Germany in the same way?

WHAT IF, ON 10 NOVEMBER 1989, the East German or Soviet governments had acted to prevent the fall of the Berlin Wall? How might history have been different?

In East Germany before the wall came down, there had been demonstrations by thousands of people demanding freedom to travel and free elections. Erich Honecker had ordered security police to open fire on protesters in Leipzig in October 1989, but local leaders had disobeyed him. Otherwise, there could have been terrible bloodshed. A similar situation had ended in violence in communist China a few months earlier. In June 1989, large crowds of demonstrators had gathered in Tiananmen Square, in the Chinese capital of Beijing, and called on the communist government to relax its authoritarian rule. The

Chinese authorities ordered troops to open fire, killing hundreds of people.

Had the wall not come down, more and more East Germans would have fled to the West. The East German economy, already failing, could have collapsed as factories and offices emptied of workers. In such a situation, the East German government might have tried to prevent the mass emigrations by using military force at the Berlin Wall. The East Germans might then have called on Soviet forces for support. This had happened in Czechoslovakia during the Prague Spring of 1968, when reforms had been ended by the arrival of Soviet tanks. But by 1989, the attitude of the Soviet Union towards the communist countries of the Eastern Bloc had softened.

The Berlin Wall might also have fallen in a less dramatic way, with the two halves of Germany agreeing to remain apart but on friendly terms. West Germany experienced an economic slump as it took on the East German economy. This might have been prevented if Germany had remained divided. East Germany might eventually have joined the European Union on its own, as Poland and other East European countries were preparing to do at the beginning of the new millennium. Some people feel that Germany is now too much of a force. They think it would have been better to have two smaller countries in the centre of Europe – an independent West Germany and an independent East Germany.

Another idea to consider is that the opening of the wall was just one small, if dramatic, consequence of the broader reforms taking place across Eastern Europe. If the wall had not fallen in the way it did, the broader changes might well have happened anyway – and eventually the wall might simply have ceased to function as a barrier dividing Berlin.

Unforgotten

" Unforgotten are
Those murdered on the border
Chiselled in stone
Their names live on
Imprinted on the memory
The image lives on. "

Part of a poem written by an East German border guard, mourning the East German guards killed by those seeking to escape. It could equally apply to the many escapees who were shot while trying to escape.

Quoted in Along the Wall and Watchtowers *by Oliver August.*

Chinese tanks confront a demonstrator in Tiananmen Square, Beijing, in June 1989. Erich Honecker had called for a similar show of force to keep the Berlin Wall intact.

Ten years after the fall of the Berlin Wall, (left to right) German chancellor Helmut Kohl, Soviet premier Mikhail Gorbachev and American president George Bush sign a piece of the wall.

MORE THAN A DECADE after the incredible events of 9 November 1989, it is possible to look back on the fall of the Berlin Wall and think about its importance. As a symbol of the end of the Cold War, the fall of the wall was a key moment in the history of Europe. With Europe no longer divided into East and West, expansion of both the European Union and NATO was able to gather pace.

Some people still have concerns about the influence of a reunited Germany within the European Union. They are worried that Germany is now too powerful a member. For many, though, the opposite is true. They look towards a united Europe as the best way of ensuring peace. In the past, disputes were settled on battlefields with rival armies and deadly weapons; or by building a wall and guarding it with soldiers under orders to shoot anyone trying to get across. Within a united Europe, with a common set of laws, there may be a greater chance that governments will be able to settle conflicts peacefully.

In Germany itself, the legacy of the opening of the wall has been a mixed one. The initial problems have grown fewer, but the former East Germany continues to be far poorer. Since 1989 some old and unpleasant ideas have also emerged, especially in the east. There have been a number of occasions on which neo-Nazi groups have launched racist attacks against immigrant workers. This has raised fears of a return to the nationalism in Germany that brought Adolf Hitler to power.

Finally, with the end of the Cold War the balance of power in the world has changed. The fall of the Berlin Wall may be seen not just as the end of a divided Germany. It also represents the end of a world held in an uneasy truce between the nuclear threats of two superpowers, the USA and the Soviet Union. This balance of power was a perilous one, but it also prevented either superpower from dominating world events.

German police search a neo-Nazi demonstrator during a march in Berlin on 12 March 2000.

Looking Back

" The wall is open...are you kidding? Are you kidding? Everyone knew it was true, but you couldn't quite believe it. We thought we would wake up in the morning and nobody is in the country. "

Wolfreida Schmidt, an actor in the Volksbuhne, or People's Theatre, remembers the day she heard the news that the Berlin Wall had fallen.

With the reunification of Germany and the collapse of the Soviet Union, Europe is no longer divided into two hostile groups. Perhaps the final legacy of the fall of the Berlin Wall is the possibility that Europe could become independent of any superpower. In this way, it may be possible for a more peaceful Europe to develop.

The start of the new millennium is celebrated at the Brandenburg Gate.

Glossary

airlift The transport of supplies by air, especially in an emergency.

alliance A group of countries which have agreed to help each other, particularly in war.

Allies The group of countries that fought against Nazi Germany in the Second World War.

authoritarian Ruling by force, rather than by offering freedom of choice.

blockade The surrounding and cutting off of a place, to prevent goods or people entering or leaving.

buffer state A country between two other countries, which acts as a barrier to stop those two countries going to war.

capitalism An economic and political system where industry is owned and managed by individuals, whose chief motive is making profit.

Cold War The confrontation which set the Soviet Union and its allies in Eastern Europe against the USA and its allies in Western Europe, and lasted from 1945 until 1989.

communism An economic and political system where there is no private ownership of property and in which the economy is owned by and managed by the state – whose aim is to provide for its citizens rather than make a profit.

concentration camps Camps for holding political prisoners, especially those in Nazi Germany.

coup The overthrow of a government.

currency union The merger of two or more currencies.

democracy Government by all the people, through their fairly elected representatives.

dictator A powerful individual who rules a country by force.

Eastern Bloc The communist countries of Eastern Europe which were under the control of the Soviet Union.

economic system The way in which wealth is produced and distributed in a country.

emigrate Leave one country to settle in another.

European Union An organization of European countries which co-operate in the areas of politics, economics, law enforcement, immigration and military security.

exchange rate The comparative values of currencies from different countries.

immigrants People who enter a new country after having left their home country.

informants People who pass on information, often in secret and to the police.

Iron Curtain An expression used to describe the border which ran between the communist countries of Eastern Europe and the democratic, capitalist countries of Western Europe.

liberal Supporting democratic reform and greater personal freedom.

military service Compulsory service in the armed forces.

money-changers People who change money from one currency into another.

national assembly A group of elected representatives who decide on a country's laws.

nationalism Taking pride in one's nationality and country and supporting one's own national culture and interests, often at the expense of other countries.

NATO (North Atlantic Treaty Organization) A military alliance between the USA and its allies, set up in 1949.

Nazis The political party that brought Adolf Hitler to power in Germany.

neo-Nazi Reviving the attitudes of the Nazis, such as nationalism and racism.

no-man's land A piece of disputed land between two opposing armies, or the waste area either side of a military barrier such as the Berlin Wall.

Ossis The West Germans' nickname for East Germans (from the German *ost*, meaning east).

partition Dividing up of a country into regions with separate governments.

politburo In communist countries, the central committee of politicians that made the decisions about how to run the country.

Prussia A central European state with Berlin as its capital, which existed before the unification of Germany in 1871.

rat race An expression meaning the struggle for power in everyday life.

redevelopment The building of new houses, and creation of new industry, in an area where these things have decayed.

reform Developments and changes, especially those that improve political systems.

reunification Bringing two countries which had once been part of the same country back together.

socialist Having the political belief that communities, rather than individuals, should own the means to produce, distribute and exchange goods.

Soviet Union Also called the USSR (Union of Soviet Socialist Republics), the Soviet Union was officially created in 1922, and was the world's first communist country.

subsidized Supported by money from the government, to keep prices down.

superpower An extremely powerful country, especially the USA and the Soviet Union during the Cold War.

trade union An organization of workers which helps to protect their rights.

visa A document or pass allowing somebody to enter a foreign country.

Further Information

Reading

A Generation Divided: German Children and the Berlin Wall by Thomas A Dovey (Duke University Press, 1987)

New Perspectives: The Berlin Wall by R G Grant (Wayland, 1998)

Turning Points in History: The Fall of the Berlin Wall by Richard Tames (Heinemann, 2001)

Sources

Along the Wall and Watchtowers by Oliver August (Flamingo, 2000)

Germany and the Germans by John Ardagh (Penguin, 1995)

Modern Germany edited by Peter James (Routledge, 1998)

The Last Division: Berlin and the Wall by Anne Tusa (Hodder and Stoughton, 1996)

Unchained Eagle: Germany after the Wall by Tom Henegan (Pearson Education, 2000)

(Video) *CNN: The Cold War, Episode 23: The Wall Comes Down* (Home Video, 1998)

Websites

http://wire.ap.org/APackages/berlinwall/story
A good package of articles looking back ten years after the fall.

www.andreas.com/Berlin.html
A personal account of 9–12 November 1989.

www.cbc.ca/national/magazine/Berlin/
A series of articles produced by the Canadian Broadcasting Authority.

www.time.com/time/daily/special/Berlin
A collection of articles from *Time* magazine, written in 1989 and later.

www.guardian.co.uk/wall/article
A collection of articles from the *Guardian* newspaper written between 1989 and the present.

Timeline

7 May 1945 Nazi Germany surrenders to the Allies. Soviets troops occupy Berlin.

3 July 1945 Berlin is divided into four sectors – Soviet, American, French and British.

30 June 1946 The border between East and West Berlin is guarded.

June 1948–May 1949 The Soviet blockade of Berlin and the Berlin airlift.

4 April 1949 The North Atlantic Treaty Organization (NATO) is formed.

24 May 1949 The Federal Republic of Germany (West Germany) is founded.

7 October 1949 The German Democratic Republic (East Germany) is founded.

26 May 1952 The border between East and West Germany is closed.

June 1953 Troops put down an uprising in East Berlin.

November 1956 A revolution in Hungary is put down by Soviet troops.

11 December 1957 Leaving East Germany without permission becomes a crime punishable by three years in prison.

13 August 1961 The Berlin Wall is built.

17 August 1962 Peter Fechter becomes the first person to be killed while trying to cross the Berlin Wall.

26 June 1963 President John F Kennedy makes a famous speech in West Berlin.

August 1968 Czechoslovakia's revolution, known as the Prague Spring, is put down by Soviet tanks.

31 August 1980 Solidarity, a trade union in Poland, is officially recognized.

11 March 1985 Mikhail Gorbachev becomes leader of the Soviet Union.

10 September 1989 East Germans cross the Hungarian border into Austria.

12 September 1989 A freely elected government takes power in Poland.

7 October 1989 Gorbachev attends the celebration of the 40th anniversary of East Germany.

18 October 1989 Erich Honecker is forced to resign as leader of East Germany.

9 November 1989 The crossing-points in the Berlin Wall are opened.

25 December 1989 A coup in Romania ends the dictatorship of Nicolae Ceausescu.

1 July 1990 Currency union between East and West Germany.

3 October 1990 The reunification of Germany.

25 December 1991 The Soviet Union is disbanded. Gorbachev resigns.

A memorial to Ottfried Reck, who died trying to cross the Berlin Wall in 1962.